Unlocking the Hidden Light

Hypnotherapy Stories for Healing, Growth, and Fulfillment

Luis Miguel Gallardo

FOREWORD BY
Matthew J. Brownstein

Dedication

To all light beings,

To those who walk in truth,

Guiding others towards freedom.

Your courage illuminates the path for us all.

CONTENTS

Reviews

"Unlocking the Hidden Light" offers a transformative journey from radical acceptance to the integration of new, empowering narratives. With deep compassion and practical wisdom, this book provides a clear roadmap for personal growth, healing, and embracing the fullness of life. It guides readers to not only accept their past but to harness it as a powerful tool for change. A must-read for anyone seeking to heal and thrive beyond their trauma.

– Dr. Edith Shiro, Clinical Psychologist and Author of The Unexpected Gift of Trauma.

"Unlocking the Hidden Light" beautifully mirrors Rumi's wisdom, especially his poem on light—where the uncovering of hidden truths brings us closer to our essence. This book delves deep into the secrets of the heart, guiding readers on a journey of illumination and inner discovery. Through its pages, the veils of darkness are lifted, revealing the radiant light within each of us. A profound and practical guide for those seeking to uncover their inner truth and transform their lives.

– Dr. Mohammed Najafi, Clinical Psychologist
and Rumi Interpreter.

"Unlocking the Hidden Light" is a profound guide that illuminates the path to self-discovery and transformation. Through powerful insights and stories, it inspires readers to connect with their truth, embrace their inner light, and cultivate a life filled with purpose and love. This book is a beacon for those seeking to transcend fear and step into their authentic selves, offering a roadmap to courage, awareness, and deep connection with others.

– Dr. Mavis Tsai, Founder & Executive Director, Awareness, Courage & Love Global Project.

PROLOGUE

Interpersonal hypnotherapy offers a profound path for healing and enlightenment, one that touches the core of our relationships with ourselves, others, and the world at large. This approach, grounded in hypnotherapy's deep philosophical and spiritual foundations, recognizes that our minds are often cluttered with "mental errors"—beliefs, fears, and judgments that generate unnecessary pain and suffering. By gently addressing these errors within transformational relationships, interpersonal hypnotherapy guides individuals to release limiting patterns, uncover deeper truths, and ultimately awaken to a more compassionate and integrated way of being.

At its heart, interpersonal hypnotherapy emphasizes the vital role of relationships in personal transformation. Rather than isolating healing within the individual, it explores how our connections with others are mirrors, reflecting back aspects of our own mind. For instance, feelings of anger, resentment, or inadequacy in relationships can reveal unresolved issues within ourselves. Through hypnotherapy, these emotions are safely brought to the surface and examined in a state of heightened awareness, making it possible to heal longstanding wounds and replace them with forgiveness, compassion, and understanding.

This journey often leads to an awakening of our true nature, which interpersonal hypnotherapy sees as a boundless state of peace and joy that lies beneath our conditioned thoughts and emotions. It is an approach rooted in spiritual wisdom, reminding us that the limitations and anxieties we carry are products of the mind, not of our essential selves. Through a transformative blend of rapid resolution processes, forgiveness work, and compassionate self-inquiry, interpersonal hypnotherapy offers a method to gently peel away the layers of illusion that obscure our authentic self.

Enlightenment in this context does not imply reaching an otherworldly or distant state, but is instead an invitation to see clearly and live fully in the present moment. It is the realization that true healing comes from recognizing our shared humanity and understanding that, at the core, we are all connected.

In practice, interpersonal hypnotherapy has grown into a global movement, with practitioners worldwide awakening to the possibilities it offers for profound healing. These practitioners guide others in discovering their own capacity for forgiveness and compassion, allowing them to navigate life's challenges with clarity and love. Ultimately, interpersonal hypnotherapy reveals that the path to healing and enlightenment is not separate from our daily lives—it is found through the courage to face our minds, forgive ourselves and others, and open to the beauty of a world that reflects back the truth of our interconnectedness.

As a graduate of the Institute of Interpersonal Hypnotherapy, Luis Miguel Gallardo beautifully illustrates in this book the profound journey of returning to love as the essence of this path—a principle that deeply inspires his vision of bringing true happiness to 10 billion people by 2050. It is my sincere hope that all who read his words feel a stirring within, a call to guide both themselves and others along a path of genuine healing and enlightenment. May this journey contribute to global transformation and the relief of suffering for all beings, paving the way toward a world of peace and compassion.

Kindly,

Matthew J. Brownstein

Chief Executive Officer – Anahat Education Group, Inc.

President – International Association of Interpersonal Hypnotherapists

Executive Director – Institute of Interpersonal Hypnotherapy®

Hypnosis – The Doorway to the Soul

Welcome to a journey of profound discovery. In the pages ahead, you'll encounter the hidden depths of the subconscious mind, where transformation and healing reside. Hypnotherapy, a tool often misunderstood, holds the key to unlocking parts of ourselves that have remained dormant, waiting to be embraced, healed, and guided into light. Through this book, you'll explore stories of deep, personal breakthroughs—stories that will touch your heart and inspire your own path toward growth and fulfillment.

For me, hypnotherapy has been an incredible discovery, one that has profoundly shifted the way I approach healing and transformation. Coming from a background in peace studies, sociology, and conflict resolution, and having served as an international observer in post-armed conflicts such as the one in the former Yugoslavia, I've seen firsthand how trauma and wounds can permeate not only individual lives but entire societies.

Through all my experiences, one truth stands out: lasting peace and healing come from within. The most profound transformations are those that begin with inner peace. Hypnotherapy offers access to that peace—a doorway into the subconscious mind, where we can heal at the deepest level. It is this potential for personal and collective healing that gives me hope for a world of freedom, consciousness, and happiness.

Demystifying Hypnosis

The word "hypnosis" often conjures images of stage shows and mind control, where people cluck like chickens or act against their will. These portrayals have unfortunately clouded the true power of hypnosis as a therapeutic tool. In reality, hypnosis is not about controlling others—it's about helping individuals access a heightened state of awareness, where they can connect with their inner selves and reprogram deep-rooted beliefs, habits, and traumas.

Hypnotherapy is a gentle and collaborative process. The person being hypnotized remains fully in control and aware. Rather than imposing external suggestions, hypnotherapy guides individuals into a state of focused relaxation where their subconscious mind becomes more accessible. In this state, it's easier to explore the underlying causes of emotional pain, break negative patterns, and unlock hidden potential.

THE POWER OF THE SUBCONSCIOUS MIND

The human mind is a magnificent and complex system, with the subconscious playing a critical role in shaping how we perceive and interact with the world. The subconscious mind is where all our memories, beliefs, and automatic behaviors are stored. It influences everything—from how we feel in the moment to how we react to situations that trigger deep-seated emotions.

By accessing the subconscious through hypnotherapy, we gain the ability to rewire our emotional responses, beliefs, and habits. We can identify limiting beliefs, old wounds, and destructive thought patterns that hold us back from living fulfilling lives. In essence, the subconscious mind holds the key to transformation, and hypnosis is the tool to unlock it.

The Premise of the Book: Human Nature is Good

The core message of this book is that human nature, at its essence, is fundamentally good. I have seen this truth time and again in my work—whether in post-conflict regions or in hypnotherapy sessions, where individuals rediscover their light and their capacity for love, forgiveness, and compassion. However, trauma, pain, and societal conditioning often obscure this goodness, causing us to act in ways that do not reflect our true nature.

Hypnotherapy allows us to peel back the layers of conditioning and trauma, revealing the innate goodness within. Through the stories shared in this book, you will witness how individuals from all walks of life have tapped into their own subconscious minds to heal, grow, and transform. These stories will show you that healing is possible, no matter how deep the wounds may seem.

Setting the Stage for Transformation

As you read through the following chapters, I invite you to approach the content with an open heart and you to approach the content with an open heart and mind. The stories you'll encounter are not just about others—they are meant to inspire and guide you toward your own journey of transformation. Each chapter includes practical tips and hypnosis protocols that you can apply in your own life, helping you unlock your subconscious potential and move toward a life of thriving, fulfillment, and inner peace.

This book is more than a collection of stories—it's an invitation to begin your own healing journey. Hypnotherapy is a tool available to everyone, and the path to discovering your inner light is waiting to be explored.

CHAPTER 1

THE SCIENCE AND ART OF HYPNOTHERAPY

At its core, hypnotherapy is a powerful blend of science and art. While many know hypnosis from its portrayal in popular culture, few understand its deeper significance as a therapeutic tool that touches the subconscious mind. Hypnotherapy goes beyond relaxation; it is a vehicle for profound healing, rooted in both psychological theory and intuitive understanding.

WHAT IS HYPNOTHERAPY?

Hypnotherapy is the therapeutic use of hypnosis to bring about change. It is a process that allows individuals to reach a state of heightened focus and relaxation, where the conscious mind becomes quiet, and the subconscious mind becomes more open to suggestion and exploration. In this relaxed state, hypnotherapists guide individuals through mental and emotional landscapes, helping them resolve trauma, change habits, and rewrite limiting beliefs.

While some may still associate hypnosis with mind control, the reality is very different. Hypnotherapy is a collaborative process where the person in hypnosis remains in full control. The role of the hypnotherapist is to facilitate, not dictate, the journey. By creating an environment of trust and relaxation, the therapist allows the client to explore their inner world in a safe and controlled way.

The Subconscious Mind: The Hidden Power

The subconscious mind is the unseen force that drives much of what we think, feel, and do. While the conscious mind is the part of us that analyzes, reasons, and makes decisions, the subconscious operates in the background, storing our memories, emotions, and automatic responses. It is here, in the depths of the subconscious, that the patterns we've inherited and the beliefs we've internalized reside.

From a young age, we absorb information and experiences, many of which shape how we view the world and ourselves. These subconscious beliefs can either empower us or hold us back. For example, a child who grows up feeling unsupported may develop a subconscious belief that they are unworthy of love or success. This belief, buried deep in the subconscious, can influence their behavior in adulthood, leading to self-sabotage in relationships or careers.

Hypnotherapy is the key that unlocks the subconscious mind. By accessing this part of ourselves, we can examine and reframe the beliefs and emotions that no longer serve us. In hypnotherapy, the mind becomes more pliable, allowing for deep healing and transformation to take place.

How Hypnosis Works: A Path to Transformation

The process of hypnosis follows several stages: induction, deepening, suggestion, and emergence. Each stage plays a role in guiding the individual into a state of relaxation where the subconscious mind becomes more accessible.

1. **Induction:** This is the process of leading the client into a relaxed state. Inductions can vary from simple breathing exercises to guided imagery, where the individual is invited to visualize peaceful, calming scenarios. The goal is to quiet the conscious mind and create a focused state of awareness.

2. **Deepening:** Once the client is in a relaxed state, the hypnotherapist deepens the hypnosis to create an even more focused state. This can be done through suggestions that encourage the client to feel heavier, more relaxed, or more connected to their internal world. The deeper the hypnosis, the more open the subconscious mind becomes.

3. **Suggestion:** In this stage, the hypnotherapist introduces positive suggestions or guides the client through healing processes. These suggestions are designed to reframe limiting beliefs, release trauma, or help the individual adopt new habits. For example, a client working on overcoming anxiety might receive suggestions of feeling calm, centered, and safe in stressful situations.

4. **Emergence:** The final stage is the emergence from hypnosis, where the client is guided

back to a fully conscious state. This is done gently, ensuring that the individual feels grounded and aware.

During this process, the individual remains in control. Hypnosis is not about putting someone "under" or making them act against their will. Instead, it is a cooperative effort where the hypnotherapist serves as a guide, helping the client navigate their own subconscious mind.

The Science Behind Hypnosis

Modern neuroscience has helped demystify hypnosis, revealing how the brain enters altered states of consciousness during the process. In hypnosis, the brain operates in a state of focused attention, similar to the state we experience when deeply engrossed in a book or movie. During hypnosis, brainwave activity shifts from the fast-paced beta waves associated with active thinking to slower alpha and theta waves, which are linked to relaxation, creativity, and heightened suggestibility.

Theta waves, in particular, are associated with the subconscious mind. They appear when we are in states of deep meditation or sleep, and during hypnosis, they become dominant. This shift allows the brain to bypass the critical thinking of the conscious mind and access the deeper layers of the subconscious, where emotional patterns and memories are stored.

Studies have shown that hypnotherapy can significantly reduce symptoms of anxiety, depression, and trauma. It has also been used effectively to treat conditions such as chronic pain, addiction, and even physical ailments like irritable bowel syndrome (IBS). By altering brainwave patterns and engaging the body's natural relaxation response, hypnosis allows the mind and body to enter a state of healing.

HYPNOSIS AS AN ART: THE INTUITIVE PROCESS

While the science of hypnosis is clear, its practice is equally an art form. No two individuals experience hypnosis in the same way, and every session is a unique journey tailored to the client's needs. This is where the art of hypnotherapy comes into play.

A skilled hypnotherapist must be intuitive, empathetic, and able to guide the client through their inner world with compassion and understanding. Hypnosis is not a one-size-fits-all process. It requires a deep connection between the therapist and the client, and the ability to adapt to the client's emotions, reactions, and mental state in the moment.

The art of hypnotherapy lies in the therapist's ability to create a safe space where the client feels empowered to explore their subconscious. This requires a balance of guidance and allowing the client's own inner wisdom to lead the way. It's a collaborative dance, where the therapist helps the client access their inner healer.

THE EFFECTIVENESS OF HYPNOTHERAPY

Hypnotherapy's effectiveness stems from its ability to work with the subconscious mind directly. While traditional talk therapy often focuses on the conscious mind and rational thinking, hypnotherapy bypasses this layer and goes straight to the core of our beliefs and emotions.

By working at this deep level, hypnotherapy can bring about rapid and lasting change. Whether it's healing trauma, breaking free from addiction, or overcoming fears, hypnotherapy provides a direct path to transformation. The subconscious mind, once accessed, is incredibly powerful—it can help us rewrite our stories, release old patterns, and step into a new way of being.

Introduction to Self-Hypnosis: Becoming Your Own Healer

One of the most empowering aspects of hypnotherapy is that it can be practiced on your own. Self-hypnosis allows individuals to tap into their subconscious without the need for a therapist, giving them the ability to practice deep relaxation, healing, and transformation anytime they wish.

To begin exploring self-hypnosis, you can start with a simple relaxation technique. Find a quiet space where you won't be disturbed, close your eyes, and take deep, calming breaths. Focus on your breathing, allowing each breath to relax you more deeply. As you breathe in, imagine filling your body with calm and peace; as you breathe out, release any tension or stress.

Once you feel relaxed, you can introduce positive suggestions, such as "I am calm, safe, and in control" or "I am open to healing and transformation." Allow yourself to rest in this state for a few moments before gently bringing yourself back to full awareness.

Self-hypnosis is a powerful tool for daily well-being, allowing you to take control of your own healing journey.

CHAPTER 2

UNCOVERING SUBCONSCIOUS TRUTHS – THE FIRST STEP TO HEALING

Healing begins with uncovering the hidden truths we carry within our subconscious minds. These truths, often buried under layers of trauma, fear, or limiting beliefs, govern our thoughts and actions without us realizing it. In hypnotherapy, the first step to transformation is bringing these subconscious truths to the surface, where they can be understood, reframed, and ultimately healed.

THE SUBCONSCIOUS AS A MIRROR

The subconscious mind acts like a mirror, reflecting the core beliefs and emotions that shape how we view the world. Many of these beliefs are formed early in life, through experiences we may not even consciously remember. These early imprints influence our decisions, our relationships, and how we perceive ourselves.

In my own work with clients, I've seen how deeply these subconscious imprints can affect people's lives. Many come to me feeling stuck—unsure why they can't move past certain emotional or behavioral patterns. It's only when we dive into the subconscious that we uncover the root cause of these patterns, which often traces back to unhealed wounds from the past.

The Role of Regression in Hypnotherapy

One of the most powerful techniques in hypnotherapy is **regression**, a process that allows individuals to revisit past experiences stored in the subconscious mind. Regression can bring forgotten memories to the surface, revealing the emotional baggage that continues to influence the present.

In regression, clients often recall vivid memories that hold the key to their healing. These memories can be from childhood or even more recent events that were buried because of emotional overwhelm. By revisiting these experiences in a safe, therapeutic environment, the client can reframe them and release the emotional charge they hold.

Case Study: Silvia's Journey of Forgiveness and Healing

One client, Silvia, came to me struggling with feelings of abandonment and a deep fear of being left alone. She had recently gone through a breakup with her girlfriend, but her emotional pain seemed to go beyond the relationship. Through hypnotherapy, we uncovered the root of her pain—hidden within her childhood.

During a regression session, Silvia was guided back to her childhood, where she vividly remembered her mother's battle with cancer. At the age of 8, Silvia's father and sister had hidden the illness from her, trying to protect her from the pain. When her mother passed away, Silvia was blindsided by the loss, feeling abandoned and betrayed. These feelings became buried deep within her subconscious, and as she grew older, they manifested as self-sabotaging behaviors in her romantic relationships.

Through the regression, Silvia was able to connect with the younger version of herself, feeling the grief and anger that she had never processed. In a powerful moment of healing, Silvia engaged in a Gestalt dialogue with her mother, expressing the pain and confusion she had carried for so long. This dialogue allowed her to release the anger and grief, transforming it into light and love. In the process, she forgave her mother, her family, and most importantly, herself.

After this session, Silvia reported feeling a profound sense of peace. The fear of abandonment that had plagued her for years started to dissolve. She began to approach her relationships from a place of love and security, no longer ruled by the subconscious fear of being left alone.

THE POWER OF REFRAMING

Once subconscious truths are uncovered, the next crucial step in hypnotherapy is **reframing**. Reframing involves looking at past experiences through a new lens, allowing us to change the narrative we've built around them. Instead of viewing a traumatic event as something that defines us, we can see it as a learning experience or a stepping stone toward growth.

Reframing is not about denying the pain of the past —it's about changing how we relate to it. By shifting the meaning we assign to an experience, we take back our power. We no longer have to be prisoners of our past; instead, we can rewrite the story in a way that empowers us.

Breaking Free from Limiting Beliefs

In addition to unhealed trauma, the subconscious mind often harbors **limiting beliefs**—deep-seated thoughts that hold us back from reaching our full potential. These beliefs can be about anything: our worthiness, our abilities, or the opportunities available to us.

Limiting beliefs are like invisible chains, keeping us bound to a version of ourselves that is smaller than we truly are. The beauty of hypnotherapy is that it allows us to identify these beliefs and challenge them head-on. Once we see these beliefs for what they are— stories we've internalized rather than truths—we can replace them with empowering thoughts that align with our highest selves.

THE SUBCONSCIOUS AND EMOTIONAL FREEDOM

At the heart of hypnotherapy is the quest for **emotional freedom**. By accessing the subconscious mind and uncovering hidden truths, we free ourselves from the emotional baggage that weighs us down. This freedom is not just about letting go of the past—it's about stepping into the present with clarity, lightness, and a sense of inner peace.

When we release old wounds and limiting beliefs, we make room for new possibilities. We begin to live life from a place of wholeness, rather than from a place of fear or lack. This is the true power of hypnotherapy: it not only heals us but also expands our potential for joy, love, and fulfillment.

PRACTICAL TIP: ACCESSING SUBCONSCIOUS TRUTHS THROUGH SELF-HYPNOSIS

To begin accessing your own subconscious truths, you can practice a simple self-hypnosis technique. Find a quiet, comfortable space where you won't be disturbed, and close your eyes. Take deep, calming breaths, and focus on relaxing your body.

Once you are in a relaxed state, imagine walking down a set of stairs, with each step taking you deeper into your subconscious mind. As you reach the bottom of the stairs, allow a memory or image to come to the surface—something from your past that holds an emotional charge. Don't judge the memory; simply observe it.

Now, ask yourself: What meaning have I assigned to this memory? How has it influenced my present life? Is there a way to reframe it, to see it through a new lens? Allow your subconscious to guide you in this process.

After a few minutes, gently bring yourself back to full awareness, taking with you any insights you've gained.

Conclusion: The First Step on the Journey

Uncovering subconscious truths is the first step on the journey to healing. It requires courage, vulnerability, and the willingness to look within. But the rewards are immense—greater emotional freedom, inner peace, and the ability to live life from a place of authenticity.

As you continue reading, you'll encounter more stories of individuals who have taken this journey. Their experiences will show you that healing is not only possible—it's inevitable when we tap into the power of the subconscious mind.

CHAPTER 3

REWRITING THE STORY OF TRAUMA – HEALING EMOTIONAL WOUNDS

Trauma can feel like an indelible mark on our lives, shaping how we see ourselves and the world around us. It influences our thoughts, emotions, and behaviors, often without us even realizing it. However, through the power of hypnotherapy, it's possible to rewrite the story of trauma, transforming it from a source of pain into a stepping stone toward growth and healing.

WHAT IS TRAUMA?

Trauma isn't limited to life-threatening experiences. It can be any event or series of events that overwhelm our capacity to cope, leaving us feeling unsafe or disconnected. The subconscious mind, which is always seeking to protect us, stores these traumatic experiences in a way that often manifests as fear, anxiety, anger, or shame in our present lives.

Unresolved trauma, buried in the subconscious, can result in repeated emotional patterns and self-sabotaging behaviors. The mind seeks to protect itself from future pain by avoiding situations that resemble past wounds, but in doing so, it can limit our capacity to live fully.

HYPNOTHERAPY AS A TOOL FOR REWRITING TRAUMA

Hypnotherapy offers a pathway to revisit and reframe traumatic memories stored in the subconscious mind. By accessing the subconscious in a safe and controlled environment, clients are able to view their past experiences from a new perspective, giving them the opportunity to change how these events affect their present.

One of the most powerful aspects of hypnotherapy is that it allows individuals to re-experience traumatic events from a position of safety and strength. In this state, they can process the emotions tied to the trauma without being overwhelmed by them. This reframing process doesn't erase the memory, but it changes its emotional charge, allowing the individual to heal.

Case Study: Andrés and the Trauma of War

One of the most moving cases I've encountered involved a man named Andrés, a former soldier who had served in an armed conflict. Andrés came to me because he was haunted by recurring nightmares and severe anxiety. He was unable to connect with his family and lived in constant fear, as if he were still on the battlefield.

Through hypnotherapy, we uncovered a specific traumatic event from his time in the war that had left a deep wound in his subconscious. During a mission, Andrés had witnessed the death of several comrades in a situation where he felt powerless to save them. The guilt and helplessness he experienced during that moment had become lodged in his mind, triggering intense emotional responses long after the war had ended.

In our sessions, we worked through regression to revisit the event, but this time, Andrés was able to experience it from a different vantage point. Instead of being the powerless soldier, he became the observer, watching the scene unfold without being emotionally overwhelmed. This shift allowed him to process his grief and guilt in a way that he couldn't before.

We then moved into the process of **reframing**, where Andrés was able to change the narrative he had built around the event. Instead of seeing himself as a failure who couldn't save his comrades, he began to understand that the situation was out of his control. He forgave himself for the guilt he had carried for so long, and in doing so, began to release the emotional hold the trauma had over him.

After several sessions, Andrés reported that the nightmares had significantly diminished, and his anxiety had lessened. He began to reconnect with his family, no longer feeling trapped in the past. By rewriting the story of his trauma, Andrés found a path to healing and peace.

THE IMPORTANCE OF EMOTIONAL REFRAMING

The process of emotional **reframing** is central to healing trauma in hypnotherapy. Trauma, at its core, is not just about the event itself—it's about the meaning we assign to it. In many cases, our subconscious minds distort the meaning of traumatic events, leading us to adopt beliefs like "I am weak," "I am unworthy," or "I am to blame."

Reframing allows us to challenge these beliefs and reassign new meaning to our experiences. Instead of seeing ourselves as victims of our past, we can become survivors who have gained wisdom and strength from our experiences. This shift in perspective is empowering and essential for long-term healing.

HEALING THE INNER CHILD

A common theme in trauma work is the concept of the **inner child**—the part of ourselves that still carries the emotional wounds from childhood. Many of the traumas we experience as adults have their roots in unresolved childhood pain. In hypnotherapy, connecting with the inner child is a powerful tool for healing.

The inner child represents the vulnerable, emotional part of ourselves that may have been neglected, hurt, or invalidated during our formative years. Through hypnotherapy, we can engage in a dialogue with our inner child, offering them the love, safety, and validation they may not have received in the past. This process of reconnecting with and healing the inner child can be deeply transformative, allowing us to let go of the pain we've carried for so long.

Case Study: Maria's Inner Child Healing

Maria came to me feeling unworthy and ashamed, emotions that were affecting her relationships and career. She couldn't pinpoint exactly where these feelings came from, but they had been with her for as long as she could remember.

Through regression, we uncovered that Maria's feelings of unworthiness stemmed from childhood, where she had grown up in an emotionally neglectful household. As a young child, she had learned to suppress her needs and emotions in order to avoid conflict or rejection from her parents. This emotional suppression had carried into adulthood, manifesting as low self-esteem and difficulty asserting herself.

In our sessions, we worked with Maria's inner child—the younger version of herself who had internalized the belief that her needs and feelings didn't matter. In a safe hypnotic state, Maria was able to comfort and reassure her inner child, offering the love and validation she had longed for as a child. This process allowed her to release the feelings of unworthiness and shame that had followed her into adulthood.

After our sessions, Maria reported feeling more confident and secure in her relationships and work. By healing her inner child, she was able to rewrite the emotional narrative that had kept her stuck for so long.

THE POWER OF SELF-FORGIVENESS

Another crucial aspect of rewriting trauma is **self-forgiveness**. Trauma often leaves us with unresolved guilt or shame, especially when we feel responsible for the events that have occurred. In hypnotherapy, clients are given the opportunity to practice self-forgiveness, releasing the emotional burden they've been carrying.

Self-forgiveness doesn't mean excusing harmful behavior or denying the reality of what happened.

Rather, it's about acknowledging our humanity and offering ourselves compassion for the mistakes we've made or the roles we've played in our own suffering. In the hypnotic state, individuals are able to access a deeper sense of empathy for themselves, allowing for a profound release of guilt and shame.

Practical Tip: Rewriting Your Own Trauma Narrative

If you'd like to begin rewriting your own trauma narrative, you can practice this simple self-hypnosis exercise. Start by finding a quiet space and relaxing your body with deep, calming breaths. Once you're in a relaxed state, bring to mind a traumatic event or experience that has been difficult for you to let go of.

As you think about this event, imagine viewing it from a different perspective—perhaps as an observer or as your wiser future self. Notice the emotions that come up, but don't let them overwhelm you. Simply observe them with curiosity and compassion.

Now, ask yourself: What beliefs have I formed about myself because of this experience? How have these beliefs influenced my life? Is there a new way I can view this experience, one that empowers me rather than holds me back?

Allow yourself to reframe the event in a way that brings healing. Imagine offering forgiveness to yourself and anyone involved, and feel the weight of the trauma begin to lift. When you're ready, gently bring yourself back to full awareness.

CONCLUSION: REWRITING THE STORY OF TRAUMA

Rewriting the story of trauma is not about forgetting the past—it's about changing how we relate to it. Through hypnotherapy, we can transform our emotional wounds into sources of strength and wisdom. Trauma no longer has to define us; instead, it can become a catalyst for growth and healing.

In the next chapter, we will explore how hypnotherapy can heal relationships, breaking the patterns of self-sabotage and emotional disconnection that often stem from unresolved trauma.

CHAPTER 4

LOVE AND RELATIONSHIPS
THROUGH THE SUBCONSCIOUS –
HEALING SELF-SABOTAGE

Love, in its purest form, is a force that nurtures, supports, and helps us grow. Yet, for many, relationships can be a source of pain, confusion, and emotional turmoil. Self-sabotaging behaviors, often rooted in the subconscious mind, can keep us stuck in cycles of conflict, disconnection, or fear of abandonment. Hypnotherapy offers a path to uncovering the subconscious beliefs that shape our relationships, allowing us to heal and transform how we give and receive love.

The Subconscious and Relationship Patterns

Our relationship patterns—how we communicate, express affection, and respond to conflict—are largely governed by the subconscious mind. Early experiences with caregivers, siblings, and peers form the foundation of how we relate to others in adulthood. For example, a child who grows up feeling unloved or neglected may develop subconscious beliefs that they are unworthy of love or that intimacy leads to pain. These beliefs become the blueprint for future relationships, manifesting as self-sabotaging behaviors such as pushing partners away, mistrusting love, or clinging to relationships out of fear.

Hypnotherapy helps bring these subconscious patterns to the surface. Once we are aware of the beliefs that drive our relationship behaviors, we can begin to reframe them, creating new, healthier patterns that allow for deeper connection, trust, and love.

HEALING THROUGH HYPNOTHERAPY: THE PROCESS

In hypnotherapy, clients are guided to explore the roots of their relationship patterns. This process often involves revisiting past experiences, from childhood memories to early romantic relationships, that shaped their current beliefs about love. By accessing these memories in a hypnotic state, clients can view them from a new perspective—one that offers understanding, compassion, and the opportunity to heal.

CASE STUDY: CAROLINA AND THE FEAR OF ABANDONMENT

Carolina came to me feeling trapped in a cycle of emotionally unavailable relationships. She found herself repeatedly drawn to partners who would distance themselves or leave the relationship once it became serious. This pattern left Carolina feeling heartbroken and rejected, but no matter how hard she tried, she couldn't break free from it.

In our hypnotherapy sessions, we explored the subconscious beliefs that were driving Carolina's relationship patterns. Through regression, we uncovered a childhood memory where Carolina's father had left the family unexpectedly. At the time, Carolina was only 5 years old, and the emotional shock of her father's departure had left a deep imprint on her subconscious mind. She internalized the belief that love was fleeting and that those she loved would eventually abandon her.

As we worked through this memory, Carolina was able to process the emotions she had carried for so long—grief, confusion, and anger. In a safe and supportive environment, she began to reframe her belief about love. Instead of viewing love as something fragile and destined to end in abandonment, Carolina started to understand that her father's departure was not her fault and did not reflect her worthiness of love.

Through several sessions of reframing and healing, Carolina released the fear of abandonment that had been controlling her relationships. She began to attract partners who were emotionally available and committed, and her relationships became a source of stability rather than heartache.

Breaking the Cycle of Self-Sabotage

Self-sabotage in relationships often occurs when the subconscious mind tries to protect us from pain. For instance, someone who fears rejection may push their partner away before the relationship gets too deep, thinking that by ending it prematurely, they can avoid being hurt. However, this behavior only reinforces the subconscious belief that love is dangerous or unattainable.

Hypnotherapy helps break this cycle by addressing the root cause of self-sabotaging behavior. By accessing the subconscious, clients can confront the fears and beliefs that drive their actions. Once these beliefs are brought to light, they can be challenged and reframed, allowing the individual to approach relationships from a place of trust, security, and openness.

Case Study: Gabriel and the Fear of Intimacy

Gabriel had been in a series of short-lived relationships, each ending abruptly once things started to get serious. He described a pattern of losing interest or feeling suffocated the moment he felt emotionally close to his partners. Gabriel was frustrated with himself and didn't understand why he couldn't maintain a long-term relationship.

During our hypnotherapy sessions, we discovered that Gabriel's fear of intimacy stemmed from his relationship with his mother, who had been emotionally distant throughout his childhood. As a young boy, Gabriel longed for his mother's affection, but he was often met with coldness or criticism. To protect himself from the pain of rejection, Gabriel learned to shut down emotionally and distance himself from those he loved.

As an adult, this protective mechanism had carried over into his romantic relationships. Each time he felt the possibility of emotional closeness, his subconscious mind would trigger the fear of being hurt, leading him to sabotage the relationship before it became too vulnerable.

Through hypnotherapy, Gabriel was able to reframe his childhood experiences and heal the wounds of emotional neglect. He began to understand that intimacy and love did not have to be painful or suffocating. Over time, Gabriel opened himself up to deeper emotional connections, allowing for a more fulfilling and secure relationship with his partner.

REWRITING LOVE STORIES

Many of the stories we tell ourselves about love are rooted in past experiences. If we've been hurt in relationships, we may come to believe that love is dangerous, that we are unworthy of being loved, or that intimacy will inevitably lead to pain. These subconscious beliefs shape how we approach relationships, often creating the very scenarios we fear.

Hypnotherapy offers a way to rewrite these love stories. By accessing the subconscious mind, we can challenge the narratives that no longer serve us and replace them with empowering beliefs. For example, someone who has always believed that they are unlovable can, through hypnotherapy, begin to embrace the truth that they are deserving of love and capable of forming deep, meaningful connections.

The Subconscious and Emotional Vulnerability

A key aspect of healthy relationships is emotional vulnerability—the ability to open up and share our true selves with others. However, for many, vulnerability is associated with fear. The subconscious mind, having been hurt in the past, creates barriers to protect us from being emotionally exposed. These barriers can manifest as distrust, defensiveness, or emotional withdrawal.

Hypnotherapy helps break down these barriers by addressing the fears that underlie emotional vulnerability. Clients are guided to explore the origins of their fear—whether it stems from childhood experiences, past relationships, or cultural conditioning. Once these fears are understood, they can be reframed, allowing for greater emotional openness in relationships.

Case Study: Sarah and Emotional Vulnerability

Sarah was a successful professional who struggled with emotional vulnerability in her personal relationships. She described herself as "emotionally guarded" and found it difficult to express her feelings to her partner, even though she deeply cared for him. Her inability to be vulnerable led to misunderstandings and conflict in her relationship, and she feared that her emotional walls would eventually push her partner away.

In our hypnotherapy sessions, we uncovered that Sarah's fear of vulnerability was rooted in a childhood experience where she had been mocked and shamed for expressing her emotions. This event had left a lasting imprint on her subconscious mind, leading her to associate vulnerability with humiliation and rejection.

Through hypnotherapy, Sarah was able to revisit this memory and reframe her beliefs about vulnerability. She began to see that vulnerability was not a weakness, but a strength. Over time, she learned to express her emotions more openly with her partner, creating a deeper and more authentic connection.

PRACTICAL TIP: HEALING RELATIONSHIP PATTERNS THROUGH SELF-HYPNOSIS

If you'd like to begin healing your relationship patterns, you can try this self-hypnosis exercise. Find a quiet place where you won't be disturbed, and relax your body with deep, calming breaths. Once you are in a relaxed state, bring to mind a relationship pattern that you'd like to change—whether it's a fear of intimacy, a tendency to push people away, or a pattern of attracting emotionally unavailable partners.

As you focus on this pattern, ask yourself: What beliefs have I formed about love that are driving this behavior? Where did these beliefs come from? Allow yourself to explore any memories or emotions that arise.

Now, imagine rewriting the story of your relationships. Visualize yourself embracing new beliefs about love—beliefs that are empowering, supportive, and aligned with your true self. For example, you might affirm, "I am worthy of love," or "I am open to deep, meaningful connections."

After a few minutes, gently bring yourself back to full awareness, taking with you any insights you've gained.

Conclusion: Love as a Place of Healing

Love, when approached from a place of security and emotional openness, has the power to heal. Through hypnotherapy, we can uncover and transform the subconscious beliefs that keep us from fully experiencing the love we deserve. By breaking the cycle of self-sabotage, we open ourselves to deeper, more fulfilling relationships.

In the next chapter, we'll explore how the practice of forgiveness and gratitude in hypnotherapy can lead to emotional freedom and lasting peace.

CHAPTER 5

THE POWER OF FORGIVENESS AND GRATITUDE – PATHWAYS TO EMOTIONAL FREEDOM

Forgiveness and gratitude are two of the most powerful emotional tools we have for healing. They are gateways to emotional freedom, allowing us to release the pain of the past and embrace the present with peace and compassion. In hypnotherapy, these practices take on a deeper dimension, as they allow us to access the subconscious mind where unresolved emotions, guilt, and grudges are stored. Through the power of hypnosis, we can cultivate forgiveness and gratitude at a profound level, transforming the way we relate to ourselves and others.

The Healing Power of Forgiveness

Forgiveness is often misunderstood. It's not about excusing harmful behavior or forgetting the past, but rather about freeing ourselves from the emotional burden of resentment and pain. When we hold onto anger or bitterness, we keep ourselves tethered to the very experiences we wish to move beyond. Forgiveness, especially when facilitated through hypnotherapy, offers a way to release these emotional chains.

In the subconscious mind, unresolved anger or guilt can manifest as self-sabotaging behaviors, depression, anxiety, or even physical illness. The emotions we repress or refuse to confront do not disappear; instead, they linger in the background, influencing our thoughts and actions. Hypnotherapy helps individuals access these deeply buried emotions, providing a safe space to process and release them.

Forgiving Others and Ourselves

One of the most profound aspects of forgiveness is the ability to extend it to both others and ourselves. While many people find it difficult to forgive those who have hurt them, self-forgiveness can be even more challenging. We often hold ourselves to impossibly high standards, blaming ourselves for past mistakes or perceived shortcomings. This self-blame can create feelings of unworthiness, shame, and guilt that block our ability to move forward.

Hypnotherapy offers a pathway to self-forgiveness by helping individuals uncover the roots of their guilt or shame and reframe their beliefs about themselves. Through hypnosis, clients are guided to explore moments in their lives where they have judged themselves harshly, and they are invited to view these experiences with compassion and understanding. By offering forgiveness to themselves, they release the emotional burdens that have weighed them down, opening the door to inner peace.

CASE STUDY: DANIEL'S JOURNEY TO FORGIVENESS

Daniel came to me feeling burdened by guilt over a failed business venture. Several years prior, he had made a series of poor financial decisions that led to the closure of his company and left him with feelings of shame and unworthiness. Despite rebuilding his life in other ways, Daniel could not let go of the guilt he carried for what he saw as a personal failure. This guilt was affecting his relationships, his self-esteem, and his ability to take risks in his career.

Through hypnotherapy, we explored the root of Daniel's guilt. In a deep hypnotic state, Daniel revisited the moments leading up to his business failure. He was able to see the situation from a new perspective, understanding that many of the challenges he faced were beyond his control. As we worked through the session, Daniel began to offer himself the forgiveness he had been withholding for years.

In the weeks following our sessions, Daniel reported feeling a sense of relief and emotional freedom that he hadn't experienced in years. He described it as a "weight lifting off his shoulders," allowing him to move forward with a newfound sense of self-compassion and clarity.

The Practice of Gratitude

While forgiveness allows us to release the pain of the past, gratitude helps us embrace the present and the abundance that surrounds us. Gratitude shifts our focus from what is lacking or painful to what is positive and fulfilling. It is an emotion that nurtures resilience, joy, and a deeper connection to life.

In hypnotherapy, gratitude can be cultivated as a powerful emotional state that reprograms the subconscious mind. By focusing on gratitude in a hypnotic state, individuals are able to amplify the feelings of joy and appreciation they experience. This shift in emotional focus can have profound effects on their mental and emotional well-being.

Gratitude as a Daily Practice

Gratitude is not just an emotion; it's a practice that can be incorporated into our daily lives. When we make a conscious effort to focus on what we are grateful for, we begin to train our minds to look for the positive, even in challenging situations. Hypnotherapy helps anchor this practice at a deeper level, making gratitude a natural part of our emotional landscape.

Case Study: Elena's Gratitude Transformation

Elena was struggling with feelings of dissatisfaction in her life. She had a stable job, a loving family, and a strong network of friends, but she constantly felt as though something was missing. She described feeling stuck in a loop of focusing on what wasn't going well, which left her feeling disconnected from the positive aspects of her life.

In our hypnotherapy sessions, we worked on shifting Elena's focus from lack to abundance. Through guided imagery and suggestion, Elena was encouraged to focus on the aspects of her life that brought her joy and fulfillment. In a deep hypnotic state, she visualized moments of happiness, love, and connection, amplifying the feelings of gratitude for these experiences.

As Elena practiced this in her daily life, she began to notice a significant shift in her emotional state. She reported feeling more content, appreciative, and connected to the people and experiences that mattered most to her. By focusing on gratitude, Elena transformed her emotional landscape, allowing her to experience the richness of life more fully.

Forgiveness and Gratitude as Emotional Freedom

Together, forgiveness and gratitude offer a powerful pathway to emotional freedom. Forgiveness allows us to release the pain of the past, while gratitude helps us embrace the beauty of the present. When practiced together, these emotions create a sense of peace, balance, and wholeness that nurtures our emotional and mental well-being.

Through hypnotherapy, individuals can deepen their practice of both forgiveness and gratitude. By accessing the subconscious mind, they are able to confront the unresolved emotions that prevent them from forgiving and to anchor a mindset of gratitude that brings joy and fulfillment into their daily lives.

Practical Tip: Cultivating Forgiveness and Gratitude Through Self-Hypnosis

If you'd like to cultivate forgiveness and gratitude in your own life, try this self-hypnosis exercise. Find a quiet space and close your eyes, taking deep breaths to relax your body and mind. Once you're in a relaxed state, bring to mind a situation or person you need to forgive—whether it's yourself or someone else.

As you focus on this situation, imagine releasing the emotional weight you've been carrying. Visualize offering forgiveness and feeling the lightness that comes with letting go. You might say to yourself, "I release this pain and forgive with compassion and understanding."

Next, shift your focus to gratitude. Think of a few things you are truly grateful for in your life—whether it's a person, a moment of joy, or something as simple as the warmth of the sun. Allow yourself to fully experience the feelings of gratitude as you reflect on these blessings. Imagine that gratitude spreading throughout your body, filling you with a sense of peace and contentment.

When you're ready, gently bring yourself back to full awareness, carrying with you the feelings of forgiveness and gratitude.

CONCLUSION: A NEW BEGINNING WITH FORGIVENESS AND GRATITUDE

Forgiveness and gratitude are the keys to emotional freedom. By letting go of the past and embracing the present, we create a space for healing, peace, and joy. Hypnotherapy allows us to access these powerful emotions at a deeper level, helping us transform our lives from within.

In the next chapter, we'll explore how hypnotherapy connects us to something larger than ourselves, integrating cosmic forces, and aligning our subconscious with the gifts of the universe.

CHAPTER 6

META-LEVEL HEALING –
CONNECTING WITH COSMIC
FORCES

Healing at the meta-level requires us to reach beyond our personal experiences and connect to something greater—a cosmic force that influences our lives. Hypnotherapy serves as a gateway to access these universal energies, allowing us to integrate both light and shadow aspects of ourselves and aligning with a higher purpose. This chapter will explore how hypnotherapy, combined with Gestalt dialogue, breathwork, and transpersonal exploration (including natal, pre-natal, and past lives), can bring profound healing and reinforce the belief that human nature is fundamentally good.

The Universe as a Source of Healing

The universe is a vast source of energy, wisdom, and healing, connecting us to forces beyond our immediate understanding. In hypnotherapy, we can access this larger cosmic framework to support personal transformation. Healing at this level goes beyond addressing individual wounds—it opens us to the flow of universal energy, aligning us with a deeper sense of purpose and interconnectedness.

Meta-level healing works by integrating cosmic energies and guiding us toward understanding our place in the universe. It helps us transcend personal limitations and tap into higher consciousness, where we can explore past, present, and future aspects of our existence.

Dialogue Among Parts Through Gestalt Therapy

In hypnotherapy, we often work with different parts of the self—our light and shadow aspects. Gestalt therapy, when combined with hypnosis, allows us to create dialogue among these parts, facilitating deeper understanding and integration. Each part of ourselves has a voice, and through hypnosis, we can bring these voices into conversation, gaining insights that lead to healing.

For example, a client may explore their inner critic in dialogue with their compassionate self, helping to soften the harsh judgment they carry. These inner dialogues often reveal buried truths, allowing for the reconciliation of conflicting parts of the self.

In this way, Gestalt dialogue enables individuals to integrate their shadow aspects—the parts they have rejected or hidden from—into their conscious awareness. The process reinforces the belief that human nature, at its core, is good, even when parts of us have acted from pain or fear.

CASE STUDY: SOPHIA'S COSMIC INTEGRATION AND INNER DIALOGUE

Sophia sought deeper connection with her life's purpose and the cosmic forces guiding her. In our hypnotherapy sessions, we used Gestalt dialogue to address parts of herself that felt disconnected from her spiritual path. Through hypnosis, Sophia entered a deep state where she could visualize herself in a cosmic field of energy, feeling both supported and guided.

Using Gestalt therapy, I facilitated a dialogue between Sophia's critical self—who feared she was not fulfilling her purpose—and her inner wise self, who reassured her that she was on the right path. This inner conversation helped Sophia shift from self-doubt to trust, allowing her to embrace the flow of universal energy.

As we continued, Sophia explored shadow aspects that had been blocking her progress. By engaging these parts in dialogue and integrating them with her light aspects, she experienced profound healing and connection to the cosmos. After our sessions, Sophia reported feeling aligned with her life's purpose, ready to express her gifts fully.

BREATHWORK AS A BRIDGE TO COSMIC CONSCIOUSNESS

Breathwork is an essential tool in hypnotherapy that helps individuals access deeper states of awareness. Through focused breathing, clients can bypass the conscious mind and enter altered states of consciousness, where they are more open to cosmic energies and personal insight.

In meta-level healing, breathwork serves as a bridge between the physical and metaphysical realms. By guiding clients through rhythmic breathing, we help them tap into the flow of cosmic energy, aligning their breath with the universe's rhythm. This connection deepens their healing experience, allowing them to integrate past emotional trauma while accessing new levels of consciousness.

Breathwork also supports the exploration of transpersonal experiences, helping clients move beyond the ego and enter states where they can explore their natal, pre-natal, and even past life experiences. This exploration further reinforces the belief in the fundamental goodness of human nature by showing clients that their soul's journey is part of a larger, positive cosmic unfolding.

Exploring Natal, Pre-Natal, and Past Lives for Transpersonal Healing

Transpersonal hypnotherapy goes beyond the present moment, allowing clients to explore natal, pre-natal, and past life experiences. These explorations help individuals understand the larger context of their emotional patterns and life challenges, revealing how past experiences (even those before birth or in previous lifetimes) influence their present lives.

In transpersonal sessions, clients may uncover pre-natal memories where they felt deep peace and connection with the universe, reinforcing their belief in the innate goodness of life. Others may experience past life regressions where they recognize patterns that have carried over into their current lifetime. By accessing these transpersonal states, individuals often find healing and closure from unresolved past experiences, deepening their sense of connection to a benevolent, universal force.

CASE STUDY: JONAH'S TRANSPERSONAL EXPLORATION

Jonah sought to understand the deeper purpose of his creative gifts and why he felt blocked in expressing them. Through hypnotherapy, we guided Jonah into a state where he could explore transpersonal dimensions of his existence. Using breathwork to deepen his trance state, Jonah was able to access both his natal memories and a past life experience.

In one session, Jonah recalled a pre-natal memory where he felt surrounded by love and light, connected to the cosmos before his birth. This experience affirmed his belief in the goodness of human nature and the universe, helping him release the fears that were blocking his creative expression.

In another session, Jonah explored a past life where he had been an artist who faced societal rejection for his work. This past life memory revealed why Jonah carried fears of judgment in his current life. By working through this past experience in a hypnotic state, Jonah was able to release the fear of being misunderstood, allowing his creative gifts to flow freely in his present life.

The Integration of Light and Shadow Through Cosmic Connection

At the core of meta-level healing is the integration of both light and shadow. Each of us carries these dual aspects, and only by embracing both can we achieve wholeness. In hypnotherapy, the cosmic energies we connect to help us integrate these polarities within ourselves, showing us that both light and shadow are necessary for our growth.

Cosmic connection also allows us to view our shadow aspects through a lens of compassion. Rather than seeing our shadow as something to be feared or rejected, we begin to understand that it holds important lessons and gifts. By integrating the shadow with the light, we come into alignment with the greater forces of the universe, reinforcing the belief that we are part of a fundamentally good, interconnected whole.

Practical Tip: Using Breathwork and Inner Dialogue to Explore Cosmic Healing

To connect with cosmic forces and integrate your shadow, you can try this self-hypnosis exercise incorporating breathwork and inner dialogue. Begin by finding a quiet place where you won't be disturbed. Close your eyes and take deep, rhythmic breaths, allowing each inhale and exhale to relax your body and mind.

As you enter a deep state of relaxation, visualize yourself standing in a cosmic field of light. Feel the energy of the universe flowing through you, connecting you to a vast, supportive force.

Next, bring to mind two aspects of yourself—one representing your light and the other your shadow. Invite these parts into dialogue. You may imagine sitting with these parts in a peaceful space, allowing them to express their thoughts and feelings. As you listen to their conversation, notice the insights that arise. With each breath, feel the integration of these parts, bringing balance and harmony to your inner self.

When you're ready, gently bring yourself back to full awareness, carrying with you the sense of cosmic connection and inner alignment.

Conclusion: Aligning with Cosmic Forces and Embracing Wholeness

Meta-level healing allows us to align with the cosmic forces that guide our lives, facilitating the integration of both light and shadow within ourselves. Through Gestalt dialogue, breathwork, and transpersonal exploration, hypnotherapy provides a pathway to deeper healing and reinforces the inherent goodness of human nature. By connecting with the universe, we transcend the limitations of the ego and embrace a more profound sense of purpose and interconnectedness.

In the next chapter, we will explore how to live a hypnosis-led life, incorporating the practices and insights from this book into daily routines that foster well-being, clarity, and emotional freedom.

CHAPTER 7

HOW TO LIVE A HYPNOSIS-LED LIFE – TOOLS FOR DAILY TRANSFORMATION

Hypnotherapy is not just a tool for deep healing sessions; it can also be integrated into everyday life to create lasting change and emotional well-being. Living a hypnosis-led life means using the principles and techniques of hypnotherapy—such as self-hypnosis, mindfulness, breathwork, and subconscious exploration—to navigate challenges, enhance mental clarity, and foster personal growth. This chapter will provide practical tips for incorporating hypnosis into your daily routine, helping you align your mind, body, and emotions for a life of thriving and fulfillment.

The Power of Daily Hypnosis

Hypnosis is a natural state that we all enter multiple times a day, often without realizing it. Whenever we are deeply focused—whether we're reading, watching a movie, or daydreaming—we are in a light trance. The goal of living a hypnosis-led life is to consciously enter this state to create positive change.

Daily hypnosis practices help you:

- Reduce stress and anxiety by accessing deep relaxation.
- Cultivate emotional resilience by transforming subconscious patterns.
- Set clear intentions and visualize goals to align with your true purpose.
- Enhance self-awareness by connecting with your inner wisdom.

By practicing self-hypnosis regularly, you develop a deeper relationship with your subconscious mind, allowing you to guide your life in alignment with your true desires.

Integrating Self-Hypnosis into Your Routine

To live a hypnosis-led life, it's essential to integrate self-hypnosis into your daily routine. Here are simple yet powerful ways to do this:

Morning Practice: Setting Intentions with Hypnosis

Start your day with a brief self-hypnosis session to set positive intentions. Upon waking, take a few moments to focus on your breath, entering a state of relaxation. As you breathe deeply, visualize yourself moving through the day with clarity, calm, and confidence. You can use positive affirmations such as:

- "I am capable of handling any challenge with ease."
- "I am open to new opportunities for growth and success."

This morning practice aligns your mind with your goals for the day, helping you stay focused and emotionally centered.

Evening Practice: Releasing the Day's Stress

At the end of the day, use self-hypnosis to unwind and release any stress or tension. Find a quiet space, close your eyes, and focus on your breathing. As you relax, imagine letting go of any worries, frustrations, or negative emotions that arose during the day. Visualize yourself surrounded by a calming light, feeling peace and relaxation in every part of your body.

This practice helps you transition from the busyness of the day to a state of rest, promoting deeper sleep and emotional recovery.

Using Breathwork for Emotional Balance

Breathwork is a simple yet powerful way to access altered states of consciousness and balance your emotions. When practiced regularly, breathwork helps regulate your nervous system, reduce stress, and deepen your connection to your subconscious mind.

You can integrate breathwork into your daily routine by practicing the following technique:

4-7-8 Breath for Relaxation

1. Inhale through your nose for a count of 4.
2. Hold your breath for a count of 7.
3. Exhale slowly through your mouth for a count of 8.

Repeat this cycle several times, allowing your body to relax with each breath. This technique is particularly effective for calming anxiety or stress, and it can be used any time you need to bring your emotions into balance.

Creating Space for Self-Reflection and Subconscious Exploration

Living a hypnosis-led life involves making time for regular self-reflection and subconscious exploration. Set aside time each week to engage in deeper hypnotherapy sessions, where you can explore emotions, beliefs, or patterns that may be influencing your current life experiences. These sessions allow you to access your subconscious mind, uncover hidden truths, and reframe limiting beliefs.

Self-Hypnosis for Clarity

To use self-hypnosis for deeper reflection, follow these steps:

1. Find a quiet space where you won't be disturbed.
2. Close your eyes and focus on your breath, entering a relaxed state.
3. Set a clear intention for your session—whether it's to gain clarity on a specific issue or to release an emotional block.
4. Visualize yourself in a peaceful setting (a forest, a beach, or a favorite place) and invite your subconscious mind to bring forward any insights or emotions that need to be addressed.

As thoughts, memories, or images arise, allow them to flow without judgment. Pay attention to the feelings or insights that come through, and trust that your subconscious is guiding you toward healing.

Applying Gestalt Dialogue in Daily Life

Gestalt dialogue, as discussed in previous chapters, is a powerful tool for creating understanding between different parts of yourself. This practice can also be applied in daily life to resolve internal conflicts, make decisions, or gain clarity on complex emotions.

Quick Gestalt Dialogue for Decision-Making

Whenever you're faced with a decision, you can use Gestalt dialogue to check in with the various parts of yourself. For example, if you feel conflicted about a choice, take a few moments to close your eyes and enter a light hypnotic state through deep breathing.

Visualize the different parts of yourself (such as your rational mind, your emotional self, and your intuitive self) sitting together in a circle. Allow each part to express its perspective on the decision. As you listen to each part's voice, notice what insights or clarity arise. This practice can help you make decisions from a place of inner alignment rather than inner conflict.

EXPLORING TRANSPERSONAL STATES FOR DEEPER UNDERSTANDING

As you continue living a hypnosis-led life, you can incorporate transpersonal work into your routine to explore aspects of your existence beyond the present.

Whether it's through natal, pre-natal, or past life exploration, accessing these states helps you understand the larger context of your soul's journey and reinforces the belief that human nature is fundamentally good.

Self-Hypnosis for Past Life Exploration

1. Enter a deep state of relaxation through breathwork.
2. Set an intention to explore a past life that holds relevance to your current situation or emotional patterns.
3. Visualize yourself standing at the entrance of a doorway, feeling safe and supported.
4. When you're ready, imagine stepping through the doorway and into a past life memory. Allow yourself to observe the people, surroundings, and emotions that arise, without judgment or fear.

After exploring the memory, gently guide yourself back to the present, bringing with you any insights or lessons that can support your current life journey.

Mindful Hypnosis: A Practice for Everyday Awareness

Mindful hypnosis is the practice of staying present and aware throughout the day, using brief moments of focused awareness to center your thoughts and emotions. This practice involves checking in with yourself regularly, noticing how you're feeling, and using quick hypnosis techniques to realign your energy.

The Power of the Pause

Whenever you feel overwhelmed, stressed, or out of balance, take a brief pause. Close your eyes, take a few deep breaths, and allow yourself to enter a light trance state. In this moment, ask yourself, "What do I need right now to feel centered?" Allow your subconscious mind to provide the answer, whether it's a simple action like stepping outside for fresh air or a deeper emotional insight.

By practicing this mindful pause throughout the day, you create space for self-awareness and emotional regulation, making it easier to stay aligned with your highest self.

Building a Hypnosis-Led Life that Thrives

Living a hypnosis-led life is about creating habits and practices that support your mental clarity, emotional well-being, and personal transformation. By incorporating self-hypnosis, breathwork, Gestalt dialogue, and transpersonal exploration into your daily routine, you empower yourself to navigate life's challenges with ease and grace.

As you continue your journey, remember that hypnotherapy is a tool for ongoing growth and healing. The more you connect with your subconscious mind and cosmic forces, the more aligned you become with your true purpose. Living this way allows you to thrive, both emotionally and spiritually, and opens you to the full potential of your life.

PRACTICAL TIP: DAILY HYPNOSIS PRACTICE FOR EMOTIONAL WELL-BEING

To maintain emotional balance and mental clarity, try incorporating a 5-10 minute self-hypnosis practice into your daily routine. Begin by finding a quiet space where you can sit comfortably. Close your eyes and take deep, calming breaths, allowing your body to relax.

As you relax, set a clear intention for your practice— whether it's to reduce stress, cultivate gratitude, or gain clarity on a decision. Visualize yourself surrounded by a calming light, feeling the energy of the universe supporting your intention.

Spend a few moments in this relaxed state, breathing deeply and focusing on your intention. When you're ready, gently bring yourself back to full awareness, carrying with you the feelings of clarity and peace.

CONCLUSION: THE PATH OF A HYPNOSIS-LED LIFE

A hypnosis-led life is one of intentional awareness, emotional freedom, and personal growth. By integrating hypnotherapy techniques into your daily routine, you create a foundation for thriving in every aspect of your life. Whether you're working on reducing stress, exploring past lives, or connecting with your inner wisdom, these practices help you align with your highest self and live with purpose.

In the next chapter, we'll conclude the book by reflecting on the journey of hypnotherapy and the power it holds to transform lives from the subconscious mind outward.

Conclusion: Embracing the Subconscious Journey – A Call to Courage and Transformation

The journey you've taken through this book is more than just a discovery of the subconscious mind—it is an invitation to embrace transformation at the deepest levels. Hypnotherapy has shown us the profound power of the subconscious as a gateway to healing, reframing trauma, transforming relationships, and connecting with the cosmic forces that guide our lives.

At the heart of this exploration is one unshakeable belief: **human nature is fundamentally good**. No matter the wounds, no matter the shadows, within each of us lies the potential for healing and growth. Through hypnotherapy, we have the tools to access that goodness, allowing it to lead us through even the most challenging parts of our journey.

THE COURAGE TO GO WITHIN

Healing requires courage. The courage to look within, to face the fears, traumas, and limiting beliefs that have shaped us—and the courage to transform them. It is only by journeying inward, by confronting the darker corners of our subconscious, that we find the light and clarity we seek. Hypnotherapy gives us the safe space to do this, but it is the willingness to engage fully in the process that brings about true transformation.

This is your call to action: **Have the courage to go within, so that you can break free and come out transformed**. Every story shared in this book—from healing childhood wounds to connecting with cosmic forces—demonstrates the profound changes that come when we face our subconscious mind with openness and intention.

Each time you choose to practice self-hypnosis, engage in dialogue with your inner parts, or explore your transpersonal dimensions, you are taking a step closer to living in alignment with your true self. **The only way out is through**, and through this journey, you will find healing, clarity, and freedom.

Living a Hypnosis-Led Life

A hypnosis-led life is a life of intention, clarity, and emotional freedom. By integrating self-hypnosis, breathwork, Gestalt dialogue, and transpersonal exploration into your daily routine, you build a foundation for thriving. You learn to access your inner wisdom, trust your subconscious, and navigate the ups and downs of life with resilience and grace.

As you continue forward, remember that the tools in this book are always available to you. Whether you're using self-hypnosis to release stress, exploring past life experiences for deeper understanding, or engaging in inner dialogue to resolve conflicts, these practices help you stay connected to your highest self.

The Role of Hypnotherapy in Creating a Better World

The work you do within yourself ripples outward. As you heal, grow, and connect more deeply with your inner goodness, you naturally influence the world around you. Hypnotherapy isn't just about individual transformation—it's about contributing to the healing of humanity. **When you heal yourself, you heal the world**.

We are all part of something much larger, and our individual journeys of healing contribute to the collective. The more you align with your subconscious, the more you tap into the forces that create a world of freedom, consciousness, and happiness for all.

Acknowledging the Pioneers of Hypnotherapy

This book stands on the shoulders of the great teachers and pioneers of hypnotherapy. I would like to express my deep gratitude to my teacher, **Matthew Brownstein**, whose teachings at the **Institute of Interpersonal Hypnotherapy** have profoundly shaped my practice. His work, alongside the wisdom of hypnotherapy's foundational figures, has guided countless practitioners in using this tool for deep healing and enlightenment.

Suggested Reading for Deeper Exploration

For those who feel inspired to continue learning and deepening their understanding of hypnotherapy, the following books and authors are invaluable resources:

- **Matthew Brownstein**, *"The Sutras on Healing and Enlightenment"*
- A spiritual guide to hypnotherapy, weaving together ancient wisdom and modern therapeutic practices.
- **Milton H. Erickson**, *"My Voice Will Go with You: The Teaching Tales of Milton H. Erickson"*
- A master of clinical hypnotherapy, Erickson's work is essential for understanding the transformative power of hypnotic storytelling.
- **Dave Elman**, *"Hypnotherapy"*
- Elman's contributions to medical hypnosis and pain management remain fundamental to hypnotherapy today.
- **Michael Yapko**, *"Trancework: An Introduction to the Practice of Clinical Hypnosis"*
- Yapko's expertise in treating depression and anxiety through hypnotherapy is widely regarded in the field.
- **Stephen Gilligan**, *"The Courage to Love: Principles and Practices of Self-Relations Psychotherapy"*

- Gilligan's integration of hypnotherapy with psychotherapy offers powerful insights into healing relationships with oneself and others.
- **Ernest Rossi**, *"The Psychobiology of Mind-Body Healing"*
- Rossi's exploration of mind-body healing through hypnosis bridges the gap between scientific and spiritual understanding.

A CALL TO ACTION: CONTINUE THE JOURNEY

As you finish this book, I invite you to **continue the journey**. The practices and techniques within these pages are not one-time tools but lifelong companions that will support your growth, healing, and awakening. Every time you engage in self-hypnosis, every time you connect with your subconscious, you are transforming your life from the inside out.

The courage to journey inward is a gift you give yourself. It is the first step toward freedom, toward understanding, and toward living a life of true fulfillment. Let the insights and tools from this book guide you as you continue to explore the vastness of your subconscious mind.

Final Reflection: Trust the Journey

The path ahead may not always be easy, but it is filled with promise. Hypnotherapy opens the doors to self-discovery, healing, and connection with the cosmic forces that surround us. Trust this journey. Trust that every step inward brings you closer to living fully, with intention, joy, and clarity.

May your journey be filled with light, healing, and the courage to go through in order to break free. You have everything you need within you—now, step forward and embrace the life waiting for you on the other side.

Unlock your Hidden Light.

Reframing and Reprograming with Hypnotherapy

About the Author

Luis Gallardo is the Founder and President of the World Happiness Foundation and World Happiness Fest, platforms that unite and amplify the impact of thousands of knowledge and practice leaders on human development, happiness, and well-being worldwide.

Luis is the author of "Happytalism," "The Exponential of Happiness," and "Brands & Rousers," and he is the director of the Gross Global Happiness program at the University for Peace of the United Nations.

He holds an MBA from IMD in Switzerland, an MA in Peace Studies from the Richardson Institute at Lancaster University, and a Bachelor's degree in Political Science and Sociology. Hypnotherapist and Mental Health Coach.

www.gallardo.world/about

Bibliography

References and Suggested Reading

1. **Matthew Brownstein**, *"The Sutras on Healing and Enlightenment"*

2. **Milton H. Erickson**, *"My Voice Will Go with You: The Teaching Tales of Milton H. Erickson"*

3. **Dave Elman**, *"Hypnotherapy"*

4. **Michael Yapko**, *"Trancework: An Introduction to the Practice of Clinical Hypnosis"*

5. **Stephen Gilligan**, *"The Courage to Love: Principles and Practices of Self-Relations Psychotherapy"*

6. **Ernest Rossi**, *"The Psychobiology of Mind-Body Healing"*

7. **Gabor Maté**, *"In the Realm of Hungry Ghosts: Close Encounters with Addiction"*

8. **Gabor Maté**, *"When the Body Says No: The Cost of Hidden Stress"*

9. **E.A. Barnett**, *"The Receptive Method in Psychotherapy"*

10. **Kylea Taylor**, *"The Ethics of Caring: Finding Right Relationship with Clients for Profound, Transformative Work in Healing"*

11. **Dan Siegel**, *"The Developing Mind: How Relationships and the Brain Interact to Shape Who We Are"*

12. **Dan Siegel**, *"Mindsight: The New Science of Personal Transformation"*

13. **Richard Schwartz**, *"Internal Family Systems Therapy"*

14. **Thich Nhat Hanh**, *"The Miracle of Mindfulness: An Introduction to the Practice of Meditation"*

15. **Thich Nhat Hanh**, *"Peace is Every Step: The Path of Mindfulness in Everyday Life"*

16. **Luis Miguel Gallardo**, *"Happytalism: Co-creating a New Narrative for a Happier World"*

17. **John Bradshaw**, *"Healing the Shame That Binds You"*

18. **Bessel van der Kolk**, *"The Body Keeps the Score: Brain, Mind, and Body in the Healing of Trauma"*

19. **Peter Levine**, *"Waking the Tiger: Healing Trauma"*

20. **Stanislav Grof**, *"The Holotropic Mind: The Three Levels of Human Consciousness and How They Shape Our Lives"*

21. **Carl Rogers**, *"On Becoming a Person: A Therapist's View of Psychotherapy"*

22. **Fritz Perls**, *"Gestalt Therapy Verbatim"*

23. **Abraham Maslow**, *"Toward a Psychology of Being"*

24. **Carl Jung**, *"The Archetypes and the Collective Unconscious"*

25. **Carl Jung**, *"Man and His Symbols"*

26. **R.D. Laing**, *"The Divided Self: An Existential Study in Sanity and Madness"*

27. **Viktor Frankl**, *"Man's Search for Meaning"*

28. **Joseph Campbell**, *"The Hero with a Thousand Faces"*

29. **Jean Houston**, *"The Possible Human: A Course in Enhancing Your Physical, Mental, and Creative Abilities"*

30. **Tara Brach**, *"Radical Acceptance: Embracing Your Life With the Heart of a Buddha"*

31. **Tara Brach**, *"True Refuge: Finding Peace and Freedom in Your Own Awakened Heart"*

32. **Jack Kornfield**, *"The Wise Heart: A Guide to the Universal Teachings of Buddhist Psychology"*

33. **Jack Kornfield**, *"A Path with Heart: A Guide Through the Perils and Promises of Spiritual Life"*

34. **Pema Chödrön**, *"When Things Fall Apart: Heart Advice for Difficult Times"*

35. **Pema Chödrön**, *"The Places That Scare You: A Guide to Fearlessness in Difficult Times"*

36. **Marshall Rosenberg**, *"Nonviolent Communication: A Language of Life"*

37. **Gregg Braden**, *"The Divine Matrix: Bridging Time, Space, Miracles, and Belief"*

38. **Bruce Lipton**, *"The Biology of Belief: Unleashing the Power of Consciousness, Matter & Miracles"*

39. **James Redfield**, *"The Celestine Prophecy"*

40. **Ken Wilber**, *"A Brief History of Everything"*

41. **Ken Wilber**, *"The Integral Vision: A Very Short Introduction to the Revolutionary Integral Approach to Life, God, the Universe, and Everything"*

42. **Eckhart Tolle**, *"The Power of Now: A Guide to Spiritual Enlightenment"*

43. **Eckhart Tolle**, *"A New Earth: Awakening to Your Life's Purpose"*

44. **Don Miguel Ruiz**, *"The Four Agreements: A Practical Guide to Personal Freedom"*

45. **Brian Weiss**, *"Many Lives, Many Masters: The True Story of a Prominent Psychiatrist, His Young Patient, and the Past-Life Therapy That Changed Both Their Lives"*

46. **Brian Weiss**, *"Through Time Into Healing: Discovering the Power of Regression Therapy to Erase Trauma and Transform Mind, Body, and Relationships"*

47. **Michael Newton**, *"Journey of Souls: Case Studies of Life Between Lives"*

48. **Michael Newton**, *"Destiny of Souls: New Case Studies of Life Between Lives"*

49. **Lorna Byrne**, *"Angels in My Hair: The True Story of a Modern-Day Irish Mystic"*

50. **Mitch Albom**, *"The Five People You Meet in Heaven"*

51. **Neale Donald Walsch**, *"Conversations with God: An Uncommon Dialogue"*

52. **James Hillman**, *"The Soul's Code: In Search of Character and Calling"*

53. **Clarissa Pinkola Estés**, *"Women Who Run with the Wolves: Myths and Stories of the Wild Woman Archetype"*

54. **Louise Hay**, *"You Can Heal Your Life"*

55. **Deepak Chopra**, *"The Seven Spiritual Laws of Success"*

56. **Wayne Dyer**, *"The Power of Intention: Learning to Co-Create Your World Your Way"*

57. **Joseph Murphy**, *"The Power of Your Subconscious Mind"*

58. **Napoleon Hill**, *"Think and Grow Rich"*

59. **Florence Scovel Shinn**, *"The Game of Life and How to Play It"*

60. **Gay Hendricks**, *"The Big Leap: Conquer Your Hidden Fear and Take Life to the Next Level"*

61. **M. Scott Peck**, *"The Road Less Traveled: A New Psychology of Love, Traditional Values and Spiritual Growth"*

62. **David R. Hawkins**, *"Letting Go: The Pathway of Surrender"*

63. **David R. Hawkins**, *"Power vs. Force: The Hidden Determinants of Human Behavior"*

64. **Shakti Gawain**, *"Creative Visualization: Use the Power of Your Imagination to Create What You Want in Your Life"*

65. **Marianne Williamson**, *"A Return to Love: Reflections on the Principles of A Course in Miracles"*

66. **Gary Zukav**, *"The Seat of the Soul"*

67. **Caroline Myss**, *"Anatomy of the Spirit: The Seven Stages of Power and Healing"*

68. **Brené Brown**, *"The Gifts of Imperfection: Let Go of Who You Think You're Supposed to Be and Embrace Who You Are"*

69. **Brené Brown**, *"Daring Greatly: How the Courage to Be Vulnerable Transforms the Way We Live, Love, Parent, and Lead"*

70. **Jon Kabat-Zinn**, *"Wherever You Go, There You Are: Mindfulness Meditation in Everyday Life"*

71. **Richard Rohr**, *"Falling Upward: A Spirituality for the Two Halves of Life"*

72. **Sogyal Rinpoche**, *"The Tibetan Book of Living and Dying"*

73. **Dalai Lama**, *"The Art of Happiness: A Handbook for Living"*

74. **Ram Dass**, *"Be Here Now"*

75. **Sri Aurobindo**, *"The Life Divine"*

76. **Sri Ramana Maharshi**, *"Be As You Are: The Teachings of Sri Ramana Maharshi"*

77. **Yogananda Paramahansa**, *"Autobiography of a Yogi"*

78. **Andrew Newberg**, *"How God Changes Your Brain"*

79. **Elizabeth Lesser**, *"Broken Open: How Difficult Times Can Help Us Grow"*

80. **Luis Miguel Gallardo**, *"Brands & Rousers: The Holistic System to Foster High Performing Businesses, Brands and Careers"*

81. **Dr. Edith Shiro.** The Unexpected Gift of Trauma.